DAVID'S
MAX FARM

DAVID GUNVILLE

WESTBOW
PRESS®
A DIVISION OF THOMAS NELSON
& ZONDERVAN

WestBow Press books may be ordered through booksellers or by contacting:

WestBow Press
A Division of Thomas Nelson & Zondervan
1663 Liberty Drive
Bloomington, IN 47403
www.westbowpress.com
844-714-3454

Because of the dynamic nature of the Internet, any web addresses or
links contained in this book may have changed since publication and
may no longer be valid. The views expressed in this work are solely those
of the author and do not necessarily reflect the views of the publisher,
and the publisher hereby disclaims any responsibility for them.

Any people depicted in stock imagery provided by Getty Images are models,
and such images are being used for illustrative purposes only.
Certain stock imagery © Getty Images.

ISBN: 978-1-6642-5386-5 (sc)
ISBN: 978-1-6642-5387-2 (e)

Print information available on the last page.

WestBow Press rev. date: 1/17/2022

CHAPTER 1

CLIMATE, HEAT, SUN, AND DROUGHT

I F YOU PAY close attention, gestures made by tomato plants will let you know when they need water. Measuring a route even—that is how I would calculate the road to success. Imagine what could be done by listening and observing. Paying attention is the hardest part, but it could be easy. Therefore, always listen to see if someone is being clear with you—and you want them to be clear. Be receptive to what kinds of weather patterns, climates, and wind directions are most likely to occur in your area. Wind plays a large part in the weather.

A greenhouse wants to have ventilation, such as a window or vent and possibly even a fan in the opening to speed ventilation when necessary. Choosing the right location for the greenhouse could help create a good ventilation. Heat inside builds up fast, so it could possibly use cooling off inside. Add a new window if necessary, because the hottest day will be even hotter inside the greenhouse. The climate will change by and by, so does anyone know precisely when it will get hotter? I don't know when, but at some time the climate began getting hotter. Scientists say it is still going to get warmer.

As the garden gains momentum, it means I have to do the job that needs doing right away, and that's the only way; it has to be done immediately. In doing things right away, I consider who might sit down to coffee and show me why I am the best one to teach. Nature isn't going to be your friend, but only in perception. If sections in the garden are dry, more watering should be done there. Go after your gardening with dedication and hard work, and you will be rewarded with satisfaction from a job well done.

After you have chosen your garden spot, add manure and cultivate thoroughly, unless it's a completely new spot. Then if your land is fertile, you won't need manure right away. To start with, any plans I made didn't hold much relevance. I could play my cards on chance, but at least if I try to learn then I will actually learn. No one can tell you what you will perceive about these things that they say you should know.

The demand for food sources will not be going away, because people need food to survive, and as the global population increases, the demand for food also increases. The climate change that is predicted will affect everyone in the future of farming. When farming methods are changed, it will be as though it is starting again. Each different method has its own specific needs required to provide the necessary nutrients to protect the garden and grow it.

The prayer will probably change; the needed methods are modified and achieved by caring. Those in charge will have to request assistance from the needed farmers, and the farmers will have to step up and meet the challenge. One who has learned how to grow a successful garden can teach those who wish to learn. My project should be to join understanding with those whose business I encounter and teach them every chance that I get. My gardening tools in the shed were purchased at a place of business; therefore, there is the chance that I could have been shown how to make the best use of them.

In gardening the result is success; however, the amount of food produced with each crop will vary. Countless tries could leave you still trying something new if your first attempts are unsuccessful, so try again. I'm not successful at everything. You sow the seeds and watch the plants shoot up so fast under the warmth of the sun. For those who are beginners, many variables must be considered. Sometimes the plants will require feeding or fertilizing, as it is more commonly known. If the plants and vegetables seem to be thirstier, you have to decide on the amount of water that is required. As time passes, the growing plants will require continued cultivating, weeding, and watering.

Big farms ensure that each crop is invested in so that demands can be met. Strawberries grow and do well at a certain temperature. Water is one demand for sure, but other nutrients may also be required. Accept that everything going on follows the elements. Observe closely and try to see how the squash may be saying "nutrition" or the bean may be saying "fertilizer." A plant will tell you what it requires if you learn to read the signs. If the color is not a vibrant green, it needs more nutrition, such as fertilizer, compost, or manure. More accurately, carrots, for example, need the exact nutrients or elements required to produce big, healthy carrots by the time autumn arrives. Sunshine allows us to see, and it nurtures the plants and helps them grow.

Farming seasons do not end at the same time in all locations. The farther south you go, the longer the summer is and the longer the growing season will last. The Southern Hemisphere has summer in January, and those farmers harvest and sell their produce during our winter months.

The richness of the topsoil is something that can be worked on all the time and improved. Strength in numbers is the only way you can have people who possess the skills to do different jobs. Expanding into new sections or divisions, such as building barns, requires knowledge. A barn usually will not be built by a contractor unless it is made clear what the job is and how it can be allowed. Often gardeners or farmers need to be skilled at several vocations so they can build their own barns and take care of animals, plants, and orchards. If they need to hire help, they will often hire a laborer rather than a contractor.

Is there really that one year that produced such a thing as a perfectly ripened or perfectly grown tomato, pepper, or bean? I think if I were able to investigate it, no one's cherry tomatoes were better; they were just boasting. But the tomato gestures may tell a different story, one that is simply boasting. Should I believe the documents a tomato would write? They would write, "But I'm so thirsty," which means, "When will the rain come?" Choosing your battles, make good food by paying attention.

Blue skies are here at this time. Then comes the heat, and if it rains, you will have crops. After a second occurrence of rain, you don't have to worry about water, but you still don't know how well the crops will grow until you see it happen. If they get water for their thirst, that is a step in the right direction.

How the sun shines for you while you are getting the job done! Which elements mean I have a good crop, and which elements mean that I've taken good care of my plot? I will be able to perceive over time how I've done over the past season, and with each passing year, I will be able to increase my knowledge and understanding of how to produce a good crop. It could be that I perceive it right away.

Didn't I realize the opportunity and accept how it would be greener? I tried to work beyond my present understanding in the hope that my understanding would increase. I found things both simpler and easier; I know it's tricky. Inside the greenhouse, it is hotter, so keep all the windows open. It's shown in that sense to be neighborly because if I thought, *It is hot*, then probably everyone else did too. Greener leaves are God's way of showing us we may have learned what nutrients a plant needs most. So have the doors and windows of the greenhouse open on the hottest days, and use a fan if there isn't a breeze. Water is so important on the hottest days, so be sure to provide plenty of it.

I think Jesus would have seen drought as a problem. In that case, high temperature is a problem because it leads to water shortages. Low temperature is a problem because it doesn't encourage plant growth. I think ahead if I can, but learning is a different kind of tricky. Use as many things as you can for learning. Each circle of friends can exchange seeds, and over time, I may still end up with a different tomato plant from another gardener's tomato based on soil type and growing location. Long ago, someone in the Bible learned to grow food—a time and place, a fruit that is their own. A star that maps out a location is therefore taught as a way that is their own. A monument is how it works—their monument.

People whose hypothesis is to get the most important tasks done right away will likely keep up their gardens' demands. If frost comes early, who will have the job done when they need help the most? They have played their cards also on the heat. Shining bright is the sun, and by protecting the crop as much as possible, a good result is probable. Using knowledgeable guesses, play the cards you have understood, but do not expect to understand everything all at once. Nothing is just like nothing, unless it is just that. Protect them at the cost of the elements you have—rain, soil, and the sunshine—most days at no price.

The sun is very hot and is an expert in problem-solving skills. The problem-solving revolves around the bright and hot thinking of the sun. Once you add the overnight temperature, you get a completely different temperature. By beginning at some point, you can make changes and improvements as you go. Count on the necessity of ongoing problem-solving, and perceive the road forward making small additions to your skills as you are able. Accept myself first, and then my confidence is rising, allowing me to proceed with building and expanding as required. Add all this together, and believe it or not, you've got something there. Capable of doing hard work, living that way, when you think all about your big plan.

Workers must be told what to do, and there has to be an experienced gardener to learn from, including what to do and how to do it. Make sure they listen; that is the main thing. To get it, it is easy enough for capability to come into play right as rain. It is probably far off in the future. Building big barns requires a serious amount of dedication. Estimate how much a water system would cost, which is again a dedicated cost. All the land you have that includes sufficient water supply and I see providing back to the land. Sunshine does a lot of it.

Early morning gives you time to perform tasks like hooking up the hoses before turning on the tap. Look up at the sky, and watch the weather. Check the weather channel, and the calculation is rain. Predictions only go so far, and there is always a lot to do. Keeping the weeds back from the edges of the garden is an ongoing job. Weeding among the rows is also a continuous job, and pulling the weeds is easier when the soil is moist, but it is best not to walk in the garden if the ground is very wet because the ground becomes hard packed. It's a busy time, and there is always something that needs your attention. Taking time to catch up on your sleep is always good on a hot day. When I need sunlight, I usually get it because it is in quantity and quality. It is almost as though the land follows a map for the sun.

Build up these plot rows, or will elements like sunshine build them for you? The effort it takes to dig the rows with shovel or fork needs to be taught in schools. I now must get used to the fact that the schools didn't teach me anything I would have used anyway. Already not seen are the elements due to lack of heat or frost or freezing temperature. When frost sets in, the plants won't last much longer. A plastic or glass cover will keep the plants from freezing for a certain amount of time. A plastic or glass cover will also keep the sun's rays from damaging the tender leaves of the vulnerable transplant. It will also protect the plants from damage when the hot rays of the sun shine through the water drops if the leaves of a transplant get wet.

Vegetables can go bad due to frost or from water getting on them under certain circumstances. The weather may be trying to tell you cold nights when it's clear or perhaps even the moon may give a warning of possible frost overnight. I recorded that on the last full moon of September is when frost is likely where I live. So at about that time, the plant depends on a glass or plastic covering—not because of the heat danger but because of the lack of heat. And it can be a danger to potatoes or carrots as winter sets in because they can also freeze underground when it gets extremely cold.

You can't let the sunshine in unless you pull the weeds; estimate it like clockwork and you will have rows that look good. Always look to find ways to let sunlight in. Plan your garden looking at all those things to keep sun shining through over the whole plant. Do not fight back against nature. Find a way to put ample nutrients back into the earth by adding compost and manure. All those things are important. Try to let it do those things nature cares about anyway. You will see the farm expand when people start coming over to help with everything that needs doing. Each time you will need more help, and it isn't uncommon to have a community farm all working together. Both exercise and work are happening. Coffee and breakfast in tune to yourself all working together and learning. Add yourself into the equation whenever you think the time is right.

Sun exposure changes by the minute, and each season the climate is different because of the change in sun exposure. It won't be able to stop anyone whose ambitions aren't small. Keep a list of items you will need, and plan your trip because driving to the store takes time. How much will it take to get it done? All of these jobs and tasks will have to happen each day. Believing begins to take shape as fundamentals are important to learn in a community farm. And who can teach me the important lessons about required fundamentals?

This farm is happening. Let's go over to the neighbors and see if they have help, and then maybe we can help each other. I'm getting close to final harvest and thinking they might want to start canning right away. The harvested crops are starting to pile up and they all need to be canned or frozen before they spoil. If you have your kitchen stocked and you can teach a helper, then you can focus on getting as much preserving done as possible. It always helps if your assistant is a cook who is good with recipes.

I want help to keep up with all the jobs that need to get done right away; add them to all the other jobs that need doing, and it might be more than I can manage on my own. Maybe I can count or try to figure out where the next big job might pop up. Who will be there to help? Accept help because knowledge will be gained from this person who is taking time to help. After I make my area that much more productive, it takes more work to harvest and to preserve a larger crop efficiently.

It is good to get the watering done before the sun gets too hot to protect the plants and preserve water. Choosing to do this job this morning, in this manner will be success. Today's action plan is to build a fence for the cucumbers to climb. It helps the cucumbers by keeping them off the ground. Each day I water and train them to climb up the fence. I don't want the small jobs becoming larger ones. Perceive how the people who are experienced gardeners are problem-solving where each person is meant to be.

His knowledge is put forth in recognition. Who are we to make sense of it?

Divide each amount of time until your timing is good according to what each plant or crop requires. Once you have figured out when each plant or each crop requires certain tasks to be done, then luck is no longer required. It should be far-fetched to know I wasn't concerned about learning. Nature will allow me to learn to succeed at getting my timing down and get a good rhythm going. Time to do relevant estimating and at the same time establish routine maintenance. I don't think it is going to be a rule to get the biggest jobs done first just because the jobs that need doing first are the difference.

In theory, what I should say to you is I didn't count any off time. I just did as much as I could do. If there was no electricity, preserving food would be a very different process. In the early days, people dried as much food as possible and stored root crops in underground root cellars. Bad weather can cause incidents that happen like a freak windstorm that blew the greenhouse over. Getting angry over damaged crops doesn't lessen the impact on the tomato crop or help next year. I think people in the Bible aren't angry people. These people are smart if they have taken the teachings in the Bible to heart. Gardening should be the big focus of people in the world, so everyone is heathier and happier. Spend the time to plan; early is the time to do that mandatory stuff. Someone else may not know what you know.

Professional gardeners have stacks and stacks of food to put in storage to be used during the off-season. Some of the produce is taken by truck to the cannery and then the canned goods are stored in the warehouse until they are shipped to the grocery store. Some of the produce can also be kept for their own personal use. Storing is a wise investment. The tractor and other equipment need a garage for safe storage. Regular maintenance could save any costly repair bills.

Good sun exposure is the first thing to consider when planting, as well as water, and then you will have a good crop. Mountains, buildings, and trees are among the first things to consider, as well as topsoil. Consider first the best sun exposure possible, then ask about manure. Be sure to use only composted manure. If the manure is fresh, it can burn the roots and damage the plants. So why would a greenhouse block out some of the sun and keep heat in? The brightness can be too strong for the plants when they are in direct sunlight, but they still thrive in the heat of the greenhouse if they have enough water. Greenhouses are the best chance for the vegetables to ripen sooner, and not only that, but you will also find that the plant will grow more efficiently.

Choose between any kind of cold frame or any sort of garden box, and I have my first of many. Composting is something that is learned from someone who can show you how to make your own soil. The chicken coop area itself will be ready to plant after a few years. It doesn't take very long to have the soil at its best when you have enough good compost to add to it. Blow some leaves into a pile and mix them with some chicken manure. Some things make better compost than others; lawn clippings can be added if no chemical pesticides or fertilizers have been used. I would pull out the weeds from anywhere I planted, then make a bit of a pile there to be picked up and added to the compost pile later. Lawns are a bit of selling your best work for good pay but not as much as the reward I first predicted from the ability to keep gardening!

Good food crops can supply more than a single household requires, and it may be possible to sell extra produce at a farmers' market. There customers come to buy farm-fresh produce that is locally and sustainably grown without chemical fertilizers or pesticides. The fruits and vegetables grown in this manner are usually better tasting and healthier. Fresh tree-ripened or vine-ripened produce can't be beat. Having coffee or lunch with someone I know gives me a chance to teach such things. The farmers' market is just down the road, and there are always people there. You might make a friend and some money if you're selling. Sharing extra vegetables and fruit with family and friends is always a good option if you have more than you need.

The time of harvest is not a time to be shy; commercial suppliers pick tomatoes green so there is no reason I shouldn't start. Heat is an excellent measuring device. If it's too hot, it could be cooler, so be sure to open the ventilation. Big watering due to big heat, so soak the soil well to help the plants deal with the heat. Be sure of the facts before you share your thoughts with others; don't try to teach someone else unless you have experienced regarding what you are talking about. Problems need solving all the time; something may need to be postponed.

Some things need to be done as soon as possible. Chill, and don't stress over it. I have learned not to stress. The plants don't like it. You want as much sunlight as possible, even while harvesting.

Feature-made landscapes can be time-consuming and expensive. Your plan is to have not a weed there. A bird bath, bird house, and feeder are all relatively inexpensive and make decorative and useful additions to the garden. Flowers add vibrant colors and help to attract bees and birds to your garden.

Be careful not to stress your plants by putting them out in direct sunlight without caution to the heat. Too much heat in the greenhouse would stress the plants that are getting ready to produce. If the soil is too dry, then in the heat they would stress out for sure. Give them a good soaking, especially in a hot spell. I found it impossible to guess what all needed doing to make the elements ideal. Even with using a regular schedule, I could be so far off. When I thought I could count on a certain schedule, then I would still have to come back to it and need to make some more adjustments.

Cold air or dropping temperature means the plants might be sensitive to a great big watering. Ease up because it may rain, and the frost will come anyway. The best thing you could do is ease up. Frost means you are almost done. Harvest because the plants won't last much longer. Carrots or potatoes will be safe for a while longer. After you dig them up and bring them in, you can keep them in a cold room, possibly in boxes and then buried in sand. This method will keep the carrots as fresh as if they were still in the ground. The carrots and potatoes keep much longer than most, and some vegetables, like squash, can keep for an impressive amount of time.

If I mulch my flower boxes it will help them grow so much better next year. Water taps should be buried deep underground and insulated, or they can freeze and then you will have to replace them.

Walkways fit into the picture. Then your equipment and tools help you make a nice, picturesque landscape to enjoy. There are a few wild plants growing near the creek that might be successfully transplanted into a garden box. Hard work fits into the big picture of the project. When you start your lawnmower in the spring, you need to pay attention to how it is running. Do any required maintenance, and put fresh gas in your ride-on lawnmower. The lawnmower has to fit where you want it to go. The line trimmer is a tricky tool. It can fit in anywhere and can knock down thick grass.

I don't see how the landscape is not considered to be a part of the vegetable garden, except for the lawn. In my yard are berry bushes, fruit trees, mint, lavender, geraniums, and other edible plants. So then my small garden becomes a much larger garden by comparison when you consider the landscape. Honeybees are a farm on their own. The grade of food they are making in one hive is astounding, as I understand it. The farmers' market is always selling honey, and I always look to see how much honey the vendor is selling at any market where I go.

The actual vegetable garden is growing the same as it did years ago. To grow is one secret the plant has until ripening. Come up with the knowledge to compare where the problems are and figure out the solutions; then you could change your mind to reason with better knowledge. I should have changed my mind right away. Now I've got it developed even more. I gain perspective each day that I am taught. Nothing to change the mind about the reasoning I have obtained.

I have always wanted to transform a property, so I've started on it a little in the yard. My relatives who aren't doing a garden are landscapers. Tree care would be learned from someone experienced. New saplings need to be watered, and they need pruning soon. Consider fencing off any area that is growing food. Plus fences will deter animals from your property. Feeders attract birds, including hummingbirds. Flower gardens or hanging flower baskets are always nice.

In guesstimated belief, I see what I perceive. Is it not about the vegetable? Harvest is bringing in the food for preserving. That is a big one, and watering is a big one. Protecting the vegetable, be a predictor who will always try to protect the vegetables; the sun is a big one and each day gets a bit hotter, counting from spring. Each day will not allow you the same chance to learn. Again the chance you have now is to learn. Each day of sun needs a different amount of water. I could water three and a half hours on the hottest day. On a warm spring day, the plants could begin to need more water. As the seasons progress, the nights become chilly, so I need to watch for frost, but September days can still be hot.

Weeding helps keep good health for the garden and plants you have chosen as landscape. Make everything look nice with all the weeds taken out. It is good practice even if it is a small area. I don't want to let this get out of hand. I want reward for my efforts. Refuse any work I do not want to do. Shovel snow in the winter. It's good exercise. Hear your neighbors. If you get apples for free, count it as landscape that you helped. I worked as a landscaper for my uncle, and it's tough.

Cutting the lawn helps control bugs, and adding borders of marigolds will help control bugs and add to the landscaping. Not the first thing anybody wants to do is cut the lawn, but after rain and sun, it is going to need doing. Things can get out of hand if you leave it and then it rains. Try to count how many cuts of hay will get you ahead. Prune some trees. Don't let them get out of hand. Keep good maintenance. It is part of the plan.

I am against crop spraying because they use chemical pesticides. Nobody steps in and makes them stop doing this. They will spray as much as they have decided is necessary. When the Son of God protested, the people in power at the time decided to execute Him. Skill happens on a scorcher because the heat will test your abilities as a gardener. Take care of your plants, and you will have such delicious, healthy food that you have grown yourself. How does one understand the example He gave to us? Believe it or not, the revelation has been passed down, and I am a gardener.

What to start on as a beginning? What if one were to expand right away by putting in twice as many garden boxes? Water them almost every day. Buy some particularly good soil, with composted, nutritious elements. Buying some hand tools would make things easier. Landscaping fabric makes a partial bottom, and it should be attached to the box. Some nice deep boards allow for depth of soil. The sides are attached with hammer and nails, and the completed structures are then placed in the final spot. Why not make my garden boxes where the sunshine would be best, maybe a cooling backyard?

CHAPTER 2

WATER

GENEROUS LIKE A good neighbor. Always be as clear with people as you possibly can. A generous neighbor can be so helpful at times when you need it most. The rural water boxes in Canada are not always exclusively owned but are shared by a group of neighbors. There should be water rights protecting the local residents' access to the water. In many cases, the rights are partial. For example, you might have rights to the water without having rights to the waterline. In Canada, it's often the case. Come over to the fence and kind of touch base in a neighborly compliment. I am clear. By that, I mean always listen and show people that you're really considering how the discussion is going.

Don't forget the time. The clock is a way to measure how much water each garden receives from the tap. Do many checks all over the property. It's easy to keep track of things that you check on, so check twice that the taps are off. By the time I finish anything worth checking, I could save myself a bundle in things I didn't have to do. In the morning, things could be checked. For example, check the tap before the garden has a big lake in it, and that way, you know before the tap is turned. In that certainty, you will have far less trouble.

Vibrant greens are the thing you go for. It's attractive. Some farms have such vibrant plants that no one else can even come close. Begging might not get you there, although I know somebody whose ideas just keep getting better. I've tried the mornings already. Actually, it's a good idea to experiment until you are doing something new that works. One farmer tried endlessly until she got it perfect the very next year. The rain could not have come at a better time, and even with paying attention, I do not know when it will rain next. There on the calendar, you could mark it down and still not know, but I mark it down anyway in case I can see a pattern as time passes.

While it is said in many different languages, how should you accomplish something that is hard to do? Difficulty is not the reward. I live where I can grow food as my job, and it is rewarding. Make sure of your harvest and a good harvest is your reward. Save some seeds and dry them, then box them up and put them away for next year. Early in the day is the best time to bring your snap peas in off the vine, and if you have lots, you can freeze some to enjoy later.

As the summer progresses, you will notice that the pattern of growth changes. Weeds no longer grow so rapidly, and fences balancing plants and vegetables get heavier as the crops mature. As the plants ripen, it may mean they need less water because it is not so hot, and as autumn approaches, it rains more often.

Plants that will grow to be big require plenty of room for wider rows, so be sure to leave enough space. You can't predict when it is going to rain, so you may need to water. Don't leave the garden thirsty. Quickly run the hose over to give them a bath. Work with nature. The hotter it is, the more water is needed. The difference between rain and nature is that it will be wet or freeze when it is too cold, even when the soil is dry.

You can learn what will happen if the hose is running. Watch the water running down a hill like it's with the tap partially on. And compare results to see how much water pressure is needed. Learn, and prove to yourself methods of learning. One main strategy people go with is to turn on the water and let the hose run among the rows. It helps keep them watered. Even if I don't believe the tomatoes are showing signs of thirst, I consider the heat of the afternoon and go back to see if I should water in the evening, after the temperature is mild. When I place the hose to run on the ground, it ensures that I don't get the leaves wet during the heat of the day. Summer is the hottest, probably the brightest, and in addition, the days are longer so the plants are growing rapidly and quickly, soaking up the moisture.

Let's go back to learning. You should be able to learn if somebody teaches. I learn as I believe I should learn, but does anybody see the learning the same way as you? Who is near to you that you can trust for good to happen, who can teach you all you are able to learn? Who sees the world in a way that your belief system can learn from their teaching? Neighbors that I trust are people teaching me something useful in the garden business so now I know how to garden. Each person I learn from is somebody I can trust. The amount of certainty will stick with you for years, even if gardening isn't your thing any longer. It may be that gardening is clearer when you are shown.

Tomorrow try to think of what you learned today. Pay attention to the taps and the watering. I decided I learned this one thing quite well. Each day I learn a little more. That one thing I learned I found to be pivotal, and to the point, and so I continued learning. So I am gaining experience to use as I continue gardening each year. This is the way; Jesus knew this when He and His followers lived as they did.

Winning will happen for me next year and the following year. Obviously manage your plants to a certain yield, and don't slow down on determination. I will make a life out of it because I choose to. The desire to be an environmentalist and grow the world's food still could happen. We could get to that point and the world depends on it. In time, we will have an answer to our prayer. Jesus must have a plan for it to occur.

Losing out on the fertile farmlands would be a large hit to what is seen as the historical progression of Canada's contribution to the world's food supply. Also, any loss of farmland would decrease Canada's food production capability, always seen as the mean.

Bets are all off. Tiny, little drops of rain are falling on the earth. That day is a good day to be warm and inside enjoying a cup of coffee. In the rainforest, it could be raining for many days in a row. British Columbia doesn't have tornadoes because the mountains block that type of weather. I seem to understand that many religions see farms as the main way of life. If this is true, then there is a greater chance that someone is growing food and may be supplying food to a community, town, or a small village somewhere.

If not the importance of the elements, then the importance of putting nutritious elements back into the soil to build up the earth. Anything the chicken eats goes back into the food supply, and in this manner, chickens help create nutritious vegetables. Some people learn by experience and observation, and other people need to be shown. Thus, the learning is spread out among us and the variety of produce available is spread out by the growing season. So it is best to choose hardier varieties to ensure continued product availability for your business. It is not only religious people who believe that passing knowledge down is teaching. When I teach, I don't consider it to be teaching because I am learning. Everyone believes the same farming basics, and they may turn out to be a little bit different from how you imagined, but I think they are learned quite quickly.

Vehicles don't necessarily mean you have to transport your crop because staying in the community rivals anywhere else you could sell your produce. There is too much trouble with transportation breakdown, and selling close to home means the produce stays fresh. Tractors seem to be more reliable and useful. For example, the tractor will till the ground and not take very long.

An earth fork will help you form rows easier than a shovel. Placing the garden hose where the water will follow gravity makes watering easier than standing and watering by hand. During the morning, you can let the hose run and let the water follow gravity, but make sure you pay attention and move the hose if necessary so the water runs where you want it and doesn't wash out any of the rows. Also, try to think of all the ways you could create a more permanent system that can be left in place for the season, so you have only to turn on the tap.

There is a variety of greenhouses to choose from, or if you have one already, it's simple. You could also choose to build your own greenhouse to accept a specific watering system, making the operation simpler and easier. Watering systems can be installed by a professional and should last a long time. I use hoses and sprinklers, but I find I need to replace them often and should probably stick to professional-quality items. You want the watering system to be simple whatever size garden you have. If everyone grew enough food for themselves, then hoses and sprinklers alone would be all that would be needed.

I practice planning during winter, anticipating what will happen in the growing season. The spring comes around quickly, and sooner than you know it, things begin to happen. Start to get things going by taking what you will need out of storage and putting other things into storage for the season. My constructive mind will accomplish more than just building things with a tool bag. Start to get your things back together, or build structures. Boxes, boxes with lids, and storage containers could all work. I'll find more than enough work to do if I have the tools.

Farming varies between soft and hard ground; people also vary between soft and hard ground, but the soft, fertile ground produces a much better crop. The hard ground is usually the area without water. If I am a person of disability who is religious, I can perceive that using a tractor for tilling the ground is better than trying to do it all with a fork or shovel. Soft topsoil means you can plant fruits and vegetables. Always remember to water your crops right; it's a miracle the way things grow.

This journal has been published as a big prayer. It is making the operation bigger, just having someone to help. A good sign is when one remembers and takes it seriously. How will I remember? In any case, I care. I can garden even though it isn't what I had imagined, and I am enjoying it. It makes sense to have a tractor to make your gardening efforts easier. The slow-moving tractor immediately makes it easier, and I thought of why it would be hard without it. I started thinking a slow and steady, easy-going farm would be ideal. Planning out what you will do with your taps and hoses should be fun.

Theorizing is a good way to begin to count or choose how you see it. Members sharing and participating in the garden can teach you how, and that has shown to be helpful.

Jesus knew how to absorb and understand what He was shown, remembering to also teach others each step of the way. The present world is waiting for what was predicted when Jesus will be King of the whole world. Then our environment will be clean, and our gardens will flourish. Not everyone was on Jesus's side of it. Many didn't understand him.

Shoveling snow isn't leaving much break in between busy seasons these first two years. Both years have been an experimental invention like a machine for digging your way out of the snow. Somehow one or two years watering my garden seems like the next season can't arrive quickly enough and it will. Prediction downtime, exciting anyway, giving count to the prediction. Count each drop of water and each season you have rain or snow. What is the element responsible for putting our garden on hold?

The relevance of beginner's luck doesn't stop there. There is a good chance you could succeed. Focus on things that are closest to your heart. I came back to the very same thing that made so much sense before. Where I go to work is at a place that has been put there for me to learn. If you pay attention, it is shown to you; it is learned, although it is also something I have noticed. Exuberant documentation is like something I would have to be in the business of doing because documents are usually left up to the people in the business of those documents, and they are held in high regard.

Shade is needed to protect anything newly transplanted, or the sun will burn the plants as it just keeps beating down. It helps to wear sunglasses during the hot season when it appears to be much brighter. Although I may be in trouble at any time a new element is present, the elements are required for the garden to grow. That's why I prune the tomatoes, or it could get wet and moldy where there could be a tomato. If I do not like what the tomatoes are saying, then maybe they are fatigued and thirsty. Rain barrels collect rainwater, and there are also more expensive systems that maintain the water available. Wells can be unreliable. Check out the water box available because one will hold enough water to last quite a while. I have a well that seems to need repair.

I may believe that I could know what to do about a given problem, but time will give me the answer. I believe myself because I know how to get the job done. I am well-off if can count a garden plot as my own, although it does take a lot of planning. And if I hold myself back by not counting a dry spell or thunderstorm, it's elemental; I can't control the weather. Can I be sure of my creek? Things change over time, and some changes are out of our control. Check the creek; it's flowing freely, and that makes you fortunate because it is satisfying for as long as I can drink from my water.

Once again comes the need for the thirsty plants and vegetables to drink, get a rhythm going for your mornings. Turn the sprinkler on, but don't forget to check it. Check that plot area to be sure both taps are on and the hoses aren't blocked in any way. At the end of the season, you will not need as much water; if it frosts, the plants will freeze. Any way you see it, grow a variety of veggies; I could adhere to a code. The way this works successfully is when someone helps, and I expect to return the favor. I have tomatoes and potatoes because I have help. So when the community participates and shares seeds, then you can build up and expand your garden.

Not everyone likes seed tape. It is for use in planting outside and you can buy it at any store that sells seeds. Have everything ready for gardening outside, and be sure to have the soil ready in time for planting in the spring. Also, seedlings indoors require watering as soon as they are planted. Start with the least amount of water required so the soil doesn't become too wet and cold and prevent the seed from sprouting. Prepare seedling trays with potting soil and plant the seed just under the surface; some people pat it down after planting. Place a table where it will get as much sunlight as possible near one or more windows, and give them grow lights if needed. They will start to grow big and fast. Give them as much natural light and sunshine as you possibly can. Plant food will keep them healthy, and a heater and grow lights will keep them growing.

Patterns are present everywhere, so that will go to my reward like the patterns of the great pyramid. Sometimes imagining forever means wisdom; it is meant to be. If I don't feel rewarded, I imagine. During the time it takes to turn off or on the tap, I would think it's everybody's reward. Numbers like heat and rain should predict how long the spring will be. It may be that when it is finally warm in spring, the soil will warm and then it is time to plant seeds. There are many ways to calculate the weather, rain, and storms, yet it is difficult to accurately predict extreme weather conditions.

It will rain and there is easily something new each day. It could happen if I were to do things that morning and water the entire crop, but then it rains that night and it's a heavy saturation. Because the temperature is soaring, when the next day comes, later that afternoon will be a big thunderstorm and more rain.

To water by hand takes a lot of hard work. Sometimes though as the tomatoes ripen, it is best to run water on the ground, so they do not get wet and split. Time saving, always let the water run for a few minutes into a garden bed while you do other work like feeding the chickens. Thinking things over, what are the chances that they might go bad if I overwater? A slope will carry water away quickly, so I will put a slope to keep it from getting too wet. When I get up in the morning, my plan is to do the best job I can do.

Melding the planting of each row is a better built crop and a better built planting. Then you have won because you built a crop. The crop winning is a science because everyone has a strategy to win. If I win, I ask for rewards because I get them in the form of a good crop. I must have watered exactly. In the Bible, they would count on the laws of God and the incredible laws of nature He created.

I think maybe it's best not to count on the weather, and I know that for a fact.

Because there should be time for coffee, you squeeze those precious minutes into your busy schedule. Take your coffee, if you have the time, and try not to get so far behind that you feel like you can't stop for a coffee break when you need it. Early is always best, but sure, there's time after breakfast too. I thought I could water in the greenhouse later, like noon, but one tomato plant burned with the water on it during the heat of the day. Some of the leaves burned on my tallest plant. Yet too much wetness overnight is another thing. That is a mistake because the plants don't like to be wet and cold overnight. Only during the hottest part of the summer in this climate are the plants OK with being damp at night. Don't water any weeds. Take steps to understand ripeness and fruition because it won't always happen as expected.

Problems aren't related to water but to forces of gravity and slopes that carry running water. Stay on top of it, and try to leave behind the things you aren't sure of by learning. Stay on your toes; turn on the taps. On account of learning to solve problems, I noticed that the bird on the fence isn't there anymore. How do you know where water is? Watch to perceive who all were in the garden. Birds, butterflies, or even wasps may have taken a drink from the puddle that is there from the rain last night. I think my point is that the rain will soak into the ground or run where gravity takes it as it dries.

Agricultural civilization has evolved to the point that many small farms have become one big farm. It's not for anybody who doesn't have the time for it. There is so much work you might find it necessary to hire paid help to get it all done. How hard it can be to understand what I am supposed to understand to make this garden work! A garden that is two acres would need a bigger water supply. For watering an acre of vegetable garden, I would still need a large water supply. If it rains, then everyone's garden in the community is watered, but I must be sure I have enough water to get me through any dry spell. It is essential to wait until seeds are mature before harvesting, and then they can be dried inside and must be stored in a dry space.

Some simple practices like cutting down the long grass helps keep pests to a minimum. Bugs can be kept down by flattening any growth where they can hang out. I would not only flatten anything that's growing where bugs can live and multiply; I should tell you to flatten it entirely before it rains.

Having a few trees in the field will provide needed shade for the animals on a hot day. In some cases, it might be possible to get more than one cut of hay. If you own a tractor and hay equipment, cutting a second hay crop will help to manage the equity in the farm. Raising animals is also a good way to provide food and added equity.

What is the best way to manage bugs? That is a decision that must be made by each gardener, who must figure out what he or she feels is best. There would not be any food crops sprayed if it were up to me. In one case, you have a simple solution of knocking down grass that is getting tall. But ants or slugs might be bothering the vegetable plants. There are nutrients you can add, and weeding regularly always helps. The best thing is to have knowledge of what natural solutions are available at the shop.

Moss can happen from excessive shade and poor drainage resulting in too much water or from the soil being too acidic. When you have moss growing in your garden, lime may possibly help, and cultivating regularly with your favorite hoe will remove the moss and aerate the soil at the same time. It isn't helping anything. In fact, moss can mean your soil needs more nutrients. Accelerate the plants' growth with a greenhouse. Use nutrients and water to encourage strong, healthy, rapidly growing plants.

Nothing is recommended to the backyard farmer except chickens. It may not be necessary to focus on bugs; you may be lucky. A strict way is not the idea; don't let anyone lecture you. Bugs will find a way, because the climate is always full of problem-solving. It is definitely a good idea to buy from an expert when you are trying to find your way in the business. You could start at the farmers' market or the local grocery store. The focus is changing to support local produce grown in an environmentally friendly way, so the market is expanding and helping small gardens find their way. It had to start somewhere, like the farmers' market. Or if you have fruit trees, the grocery store could buy your fruit. It just has to be good food.

Prepare a long way into the future if you expect to grow a successful market garden. So in the greenhouse, you're doing your part to keep the plants healthy and fertilized with manure. Buy the seeds that are essential to your plans. Provide your fruit trees the necessary water and nutrients, and you will have a healthy and productive orchard. Know-how is always good when picking things up at the store. Problem-solving is also a great help. A contractor is good at picking up the essential supplies and construction materials and getting the best deal possible from the store owner.

Problem-solving in this journal is written in the most basic way I could find. The season's end brings a drastic change to the weather, even in the greenhouse. It's cold at night, bringing a change to the day's sun. The day's sun is always changing throughout the year. Water temperature will be colder unless you are heating it for some reason. And freezing water can only mean it is time. In British Columbia, we get a lot of rain—and a lot of snow in the winter. There are a lot of people growing food on my road, and that includes me. Changing temperatures predict the end of the growing season, although garlic is planted in the fall, stays dormant over the winter, and then starts to grow in early spring. Asparagus is another vegetable that is dormant through the winter and then grows very early in the spring.

The buyer of the property is prepared for this. Water is the first priority. Prepare twice to understand the property water. When making a property purchase, you will also want to choose the very best sun exposure for your garden. Do you have an acreage that is subject to flooding in the spring? Or how often do you need to apply drainage? Have someone divert water drainage if you think you need to. Check into the history of the property. Maybe, if you ask, the Realtor knows some things about your property's water.

CHAPTER 3

VEGETABLES

IF REALLY NOTHING in a big way seemed to follow your calculated model, don't worry about it. If peas take up space near the beets or carrots, then there could have been less work building up the raised rows if you left more room between them. Nothing short of good composure, except squash, will grow all over the place and grow up a fence. These vegetables will climb a fence so they are growing vertically, which makes the most of the space and leaves the path clear. Green beans, butternut squash, cucumber, peas, and tomatoes will all grow up a fence, and that keeps them off the ground, making it easier to prune them and pick them. Being off the ground also protects them from some pests.

Realize nice, clean, evenly spaced rows and even paths. Once you do that, make great, big predictions planning the best place for each vegetable row, depending upon depth of soil, need for water, and exposure to sunshine. It sounds easy, but it can be tricky getting the water to every corner of the garden. I found that creating the raised rows widthwise across the garden made it a lot easier to get the hoses delivering the water to all areas of the garden as required. Later in the year, it will end up saving you time because the plants grow big and fast. It is also best to keep the tallest plants located where they won't shade the shorter ones.

Hill up the potato plants to make sure the potatoes are covered so they don't go green from exposure to sunlight. Continue hilling to make a deeper potato bed to get even more potatoes. Seed potatoes are from last year and are making shoots because they've gone to seed. Potatoes need lots of water and can be grown with corn because corn also needs to be well watered. Carrots need quite a bit of water and can grow well with peas; peas like it when it rains a lot. Zucchini does not like to be kept wet in the fall, and it is done when it frosts or freezes. Radish and lettuce will shoot up and go to seed when it gets hot. Carrots don't go to seed until the following year.

Fruit trees count as equity and will require watering and possibly additional nutrients from manure or compost when first planted in a new location. Keep records in case you need to explain to another caregiver what needs to be done. If it is a hot, dry year, more watering will be required. It is important to learn the correct way to prune the young trees.

I didn't have to guess how to calculate the plot because I was being taught. Once you are on your third year, you are in a better position to decide where to plant. I wouldn't try a completely new approach. I would for the most part follow the blueprints from the previous year. If you feel like it's a comedy, don't be concerned. I just think of it as planting out the garden plot. What a professional farmer will do is grow to scale. He won't be worried or concerned about where this or that is located unless he needs to know for a particular task.

When you first transplant any previously started plants that haven't been outside already, they will need to be protected with plastic or glass and gradually introduced to direct sunshine and lower temperatures at night. Dry plastic works so much better to place over U-shaped supports to protect the plants and protect your work during spring, summer, and fall. If somebody showed you glazing, then they would say there is more than one use. Transplanting is an essential use for keeping things out as well as keeping things in. The greenhouse is an essential use. It protects the plants from cold weather and frost. It provides extra warmth and humidity and protects from rain when the tomatoes are getting ripe. The end result is that it makes the plants grow so much faster.

Problem-solvers accepting problems to solve will result in success, and without them, tasks would be very hard. Owning a tractor makes a huge difference when it comes time to till the garden. Expansion projects bring new challenges. It is hard to understand what is required when you haven't grown asparagus before. It is not something that is planted from seed each year. The asparagus plants grow fresh shoots each year, and that is the part that is harvested and eaten, but prior to harvesting many shoots, the plants need to be established. They must be weeded and watered in spring and summer and mulched in the fall to protect them from freezing. As the plants become established, they will produce a larger crop of asparagus shoots. People trying to do it on their own will probably find they need to be shown. Throw the plastic on them to tuck them in at night, but remember to ventilate during the next day's sunshine.

The climate and the weather provide the reason for a fast-growing crop; the sun and everything else make fast growth occur after rain because nutrients and water are delivered straight to the root. All the essential nutrients must be present, not that you didn't know that already. So there are at least three parts: the root, the vegetable, and the gardener. A warm temperature is one of the most important things when it comes to growing.

The word *essential* means that without the elements, you cannot cause growth to occur. Adding the list of as many essential elements as exist in nature could be as long as a book itself. There should be shops that work with the local gardeners no matter what. Every acre of farming could mean that there may not be a shortage of food. The world's gardens should fill up as much of the world as it takes to grow enough food for everyone. In the Bible, the words that you speak should be helpful in teaching others to be kind to the earth and her nature. Every acre farmed would mean that much more food. It takes more than the world; it takes people.

Throughout history, people would try to grow food and usually succeed. Growers could have enough food to trade with others. They could make it on just one acre of land and have their friends come to help so each helper would share in the food grown. Basically, the earth could sustain itself and have all the food needed if there were more farms and gardens and more people spent time working them. Once that happens, the carbon footprint will be reduced to much less than it is at present.

If you water very well, you will have a successful transplant. My only regret is not whether I paid enough attention but that I could have learned more by talking to more people. If I remember to network with relatives, I can share my produce with them and try their produce. Early season or late season, it makes an excellent time to learn what I can from someone.

As the gardening season progresses, potential problems are endless because the plants keep getting heavier. Fences have to balance tomatoes as autumn is getting closer. When the fruit or vegetable is getting ripe, you need to watch closely and check them daily to determine when they are ready to pick. Be sure to give yourself enough time to get the whole crop harvested. It is also important to watch for rain as many ripe fruits and tomatoes can be damaged by rain. There isn't any expendable time. Spendable time in this business is time spent.

Picking some vegetables is acceptable to the plant, but if you pick all the vegetables, you might inadvertently teach the plant that it is finished. Early on, some will ripen, and others will follow. Peas are one of the first crops to ripen, and once they are ripe, it is time to pick. They need to be picked at just the right stage of ripeness. Bring them inside, and preserve them by canning or freezing. Bring the crop inside, and turn on the kitchen. When it comes to tomatoes and peppers, they will continue to ripen after being picked. Store them in wooden or cardboard flats, and keep an eye on them so they don't go bad. Check them daily, and preserve the ones that are ripe.

When it is supposed to occur, there will be lovely new tomatoes of the variety that best suits you. It can't happen until then, even though you work on it all season long until then. The final stage and then you have all those things on the shelf waiting for you. I begin to have the crop harvest, and it happens fast—canning and preserving as fast as I can and eating zucchini fritters for breakfast every day. I am a guesser when it's bringing in the harvested vegetables. When picking green tomatoes, grocery stores know exactly when to pick them. Check potatoes for ones that have spots and discard those. Potatoes must be kept in a cool, dark place free of dampness. Apples can last for weeks just sitting on the counter, but storing them in a cold room is even better. I make lots of dried apples and applesauce and then can some of the applesauce. Ask for somebody to show you knowledge, because I think a successful farmer would have had somebody to show him the knowledge he needed. How would you know what to do if nobody showed you?

It takes everything the boss has got to run a big operation. He knows everything that has been done there, including everything that goes into it and who gets paid. The workers' wages were probably a small amount in comparison to how much the food is worth. At least that is the outcome the farmer is hoping to achieve. Consumers buy everything they need from the grocery store where the produce is sold. So if the economy was based on local shops, then they would be what supports the community.

Done in the right order, predicting and calculating can make things work. Count each of the plot rows and each of the plot fences to arrange them in an order that will work well. Clear away any kinds of weeds or growth anywhere in the general area where the seeds will be planted. Tall grass can be knocked down using a trimmer. Try to remember to use your compost pile anywhere you can, all to keep the produce to taste.

Relying on one main belief while putting up the fences, count the plot to come together as a simple math. This means that once the vegetable supports are up, it should be easy to train them to climb the fence. It seems tricky until the cucumber starts to climb up the fence, building on to your expectations to train it. So that means you are building on to the area you are planting. Increase your weed control efforts after the rain, and plan to water with a good soaking when it is hot.

Honoring the ideas that I come up with isn't easy. Some of the fruits and vegetables go bad so they have to go to the chickens. The neighbor's apples are good, and I'm hoping I have something they would like to trade for them. From one year to the next, the size of the crop will vary. If there is a late frost when the trees are in bloom, the frost will kill the buds and the fruit won't grow, causing the grower to lose the crop.

Be a study to someone who is trustworthy and is in possession of agricultural experience. I didn't know it to see it, but this is how it works. The water I provided for the plants to grow every morning is to try to make them begin to ripen before the end of the season. The greenhouse helps the plants grow faster so I will have ripe tomatoes sooner. After the crop is harvested in the fall, the ground can be tilled before it sits dormant for the winter.

When it is raining, it is time to relax or take a nap unless there is work you could do in the greenhouse. Early hours are the time to get things done, unless you are busy working on it all the time. Because you are in on it all the time, you know when the peppers and tomatoes thirst.

Butternut squash will grow as many as you are willing to plant; tomatoes could grow more than you have time to preserve in jars. I grow my variety because I understand them or because they are hardy. The tomato has to be secured to something above, then trim back or prune any extra growth. Somehow the variety won't let you know right away what will happen. How early will I need to prune? If you want the plants to grow tall, supported off the ground, you should trim any shoots that want to become branches. Then the plant can focus on producing tomatoes. Peppers in the greenhouse like lots of water and pair well with tomatoes. To make it the best you can, it's teachable.

Later in time, I have my food canned or preserved then keep my share where I know where it is, including pears, plums, and apples. Every day I check the storage boxes to see if any of the fruit is starting to spoil. Hard work can seem like you are doing a lot when you are not, so look for rewards. The Bible teaches us that rest is your reward for a hard day's work. Make an action plan over the winter while there is not as much work to do outside. I have my hay below a roof. In this manner, it is there when I need it because I have many uses for it and wet hay goes bad. Ending in success, everything is done for the day and the animals are fed.

All the ways I count on things I do well, things like prayer. I know I can count on the Lord in prayer. Unless I have not made up my mind yet how to do good. Consider bringing help, almost like an expansion of operation. Tomato picking on its own could take hours. Don't pick all of them at once. Start with the ripest ones. I have been making progress each step of the way, and it means I cannot be sure of the result, but I continue to work toward a good outcome next year. But the taps are off for the winter. Insulate the asparagus, take apart the garden fences, and clear the garden so it is ready for tilling; teaching and learning mean progress.

Examples of preparedness are as follows: You can be up in the morning; the required watering must always be done. Make time for coffee, if it is close to your heart. How does a skill apply to the real world? Is it the fundamental of the real world? How do I understand real-world problem-solving, including canning storage, freezer storing solutions, cold room design, and shelving off the floor? Inside, start seeds early, transplanting outdoors or taking them to the greenhouse. Then at the end of the growing season, take them back inside and prepare them for storage.

The need for one rain after another belongs in the rainforest. Getting more sun belongs with growing food in this climate. And tomatoes, carrots, squash, and zucchini are several that I know how to grow because I'm Canadian. Counting on it to be sunny or counting on the rain should be predicted or simple. One could predict it to be rainy or one could count on it being sunny. Paying more attention, continuously the weather changes, so that means the good elements were predicted. My favorite neighbor for zucchini is butternut squash and cucumber, so you know how much effort went into watering.

They taste just as good as one another any way they are preserved—cookbook recipe or right off the vine. Storage isn't making them any less good. One big upside is how long they will last on the shelf once they are canned. Grocery stores should be packed full of any produce and sold out should be the next thing. Cold or heated peaches, peach jam, or peaches made into a recipe—there had to be a way to preserve them in a means to contain their essence. And a long time ago, they invented burying the potato and carrot in sand in the root cellar so the shelf life would be extended greatly. Just keeping it cool or away from light and moisture helps it store better.

Where do you want to be in a few years? A small operation is the most acceptable for beginners. Beginners should start as students. Big farms employ workers, and a lot of the time, they are migrant workers. Trading food is a good way to start building a network. Likely you would have done networking when you started out; it's what I'm doing. Try to count how much work is acceptable for me, so I then can make a doable plan. There must be a way to foresee, after one year of doing it. I have a way to foresee a second year and a second way to foresee. Water, sun, and soil will play major decision-making factors in your action plan to plant the best possible square footage of plants. Garden areas spread out over a larger area will take up a considerably larger amount of time. Some plants will block the sun from other plants, and the idea is to lay out your garden in a way that will keep that from happening.

There is not a time when you shouldn't be gardening, am I not right? To grow food is to listen to God. Believing is the one true fundamental. How is the earth connected by the main one? And the connection with the earth is the main one to know. Praying, food comes from the earth and the connection to the earth plays a role. It comes down to praying there is food from the garden. Let's face it: it is better when you grow your own.

Something I have learned a lot is why they will not listen to an agenda; people will only listen to their own agenda. Except before you even think it, they are hearing. Listening means paying attention so that means hearing agendas. Their best, busiest day is the family farm because just like that, it is their family food business.

Be prevalent in the sense of how you are in charge and the circle of friends understand each other. Prevail to be understood where others can't be understood, and that is good enough. What will I be able to learn, and who will teach me to be as big as anyone? In one aspect of the day, I can have knowledge that applies. So if I keep harvesting my own seeds, my plants will adapt and acclimatize themselves to the specific conditions of their surroundings. Right away, it is resulting in a certain kind of produce, and it grows in a certain way. It is simple.

When should a hose never be left running? When do you move the hose if you are running it somewhere? Only leave the hose running because the water is doing a good job for how much time it is running. Garden boxes should have drainage, and think of all the berries you could have! Wouldn't it be great if you added on a flower garden to help attract the bees? Keep adding on to the flower gardens around the property. The more times something is transplanted, the more you expose the root. Young plants, like at any other age, need water, so measure the fertilizer carefully and get it right from the beginning. There are a lot of different varieties to choose from. Pick some bee-friendly flowers to attract the bees to the garden because they are essential for pollenating the plants to make them produce fruit. It might be a good thing to take a bee course.

Any day now, it could be above-average temperature, and any day now, it could be below-average temperature, but if the plants are even a little thirsty today, that's still eventful. New garden space, new fences surrounding the garden space, and fences to train the plants to climb. I would have several greenhouses if I were going to expand my operations because there are many ways that a greenhouse is better for gardening.

The first one ready for use is usually the lettuce because it grows quickly, and it needs to be used before it goes to seed. By that I mean you should grow the variety you have chosen but know how they will grow so you are prepared to make the most use of them. Other varieties, like chard, kale, and spinach, grow in a similar manner, but lettuce was the one I chose for my garden. I think I will add more variety this year. Remember when someone is explaining about lettuce or radish. They need to be picked as soon as they are ready to keep them from getting overripe, but they taste good chilling in the fridge.

I could guess my way through it. Counting will do more than guessing and I've been at it for a couple of years. If a time limit would happen, I would feel rewarded by using my own timeline. Multiple hours a day might be just a start the way you or I see it. Working out a suitable garden site is different from mapping your own. In what ways are you putting back into the soil? Education courses will teach how to garden and landscape and also provide knowledge for building up and improving the quality of the soil.

All right, it is morning, and it is out to the garden to start the day by looking around and checking on things before turning the water on. Check to be sure the support fences are secure as the vegetables are getting heavier each day. Or maybe you are on to your next level and your fences are secure. The sunlight isn't the only best thing for it. Having a greenhouse makes the sunshine and growing conditions even better, but you must open the doors and windows early on a hot day. If you read the temperature in the greenhouse and add a window, you can still close the door if necessary.

In one season versus another season, making wide paths and wide rows didn't compare to having the rows perpendicular to the water supply, making watering a whole lot easier.

When butternut squash is trained to grow vertically, it will climb the fence, but it will also grow branches in all different directions. Zucchini can balance on the ground and squash will too, but other varieties of squash will grow up a fence, thus keeping it off the ground and out of any puddles of water.

Canning

Take the rainy days off from the garden and spend your time in the kitchen preserving all the best fruits and vegetables by canning them or freezing them. Then you can take some of the leftover fruits and vegetables to make juice. If you have an abundance of vegetables or fruit, you can use them to make juice on a regular basis as a nutritious boost to your diet. The thing about making juice is that you will have to wash the juicer often. Making jam is also a good way to use leftover fruit.

Divide the tomatoes to lie flat in one layer, and check them regularly to be sure that they are not going bad.

It is also a good idea to keep soft fruits like peaches, pears, and plums in a single layer while they ripen enough for canning. An equal amount of sugar per amount of fruit is an approximate amount for making jam, and an equal amount of vinegar per water is an average amount for making pickling brine. Freezing is one easy way to preserve your fruits and vegetables.

Water bath canning is the way I prefer to do my canning. Some things like cherries are simple to can because they don't need to be peeled or chopped. I just wash them, put them into the jar, and fill the jar with hot water or syrup, which is just water with some sugar added. The syrup can have just a bit of sugar or more if you prefer your fruit sweeter. The jars are then added to a canner full of hot water. Plums can be done the same way. Peaches and pears are best when peeled, cored, or pitted and sliced. That means a lot more work, but it is worth it because they are so good.

Dill pickles are similar because they just need to be washed and packed into hot jars and then covered with pickling brine before being put into the canner full of water and processed. The time in the canner is about half an hour for fruit and ten or fifteen minutes for pickles, but following a recipe for exactly what you are doing is best. Processing time varies, depending on what you are canning, what size jar you are using, and what the elevation is where you live. Green beans can be done the same way as dill pickles, and they are a favorite in my family.

Salsa, relish, and tomato sauce are all delicious homemade foods, but they are a lot more work. Peeling the tomatoes and chopping the vegetables is time-consuming, although using a food processor does help speed things along. All the delicious, homegrown, and home-canned food is a source of great reward and enjoyment throughout the winter months.

CHAPTER 4

ANIMALS

PLANS TO BUILD barns could be a bigger job than you are ready to take on, so ask yourself if it's too soon for that. Building below the hill isn't out of the question. For example, digging a root cellar into the side of the hill could create useful storage space for your root crops. Hiring a worker isn't out of the question if you can afford it. Costs must be considered before you move forward with the plans. Consider ways you can make use of what you have by conducting repairs on existing buildings to save money and build fences around them so they can be used for animal shelter. For example, that old garden shed has a solid framework, so replacing the interior and exterior paneling will make a good chicken coop. Keep a good head about communicating with people you know because barns or buildings are likely costly and a big expense.

Plan on buying the building materials and probably paying someone to build a small barn or storage shed that you can temporarily keep animals in. The main way to protect the animals is to raise them away from the cold rain and snow and away from any predators, such as coyotes or bears. If you have a problem with predators, electric fencing is one way to keep them away from your animals. When you look at the main concern with food production, consider how will it be to raise animals for your own food. Once you have spent the money to produce chicken eggs from your hens, they will need food and water every day and a suitable shelter to keep them safe. In winter, you will need to keep them warm and keep their water from freezing.

The simplest way of maintaining the hay field is to have it cut, or animals could be pastured on the fields and eat it, but then you would have to buy enough hay for the winter. Animals will eat any weeds too. A second cutting and baling will work if the field is watered. If the hay is growing again after the first cut, then water it if you're trying to make a second cut. The hay equipment needs a heavy-duty tractor to pull the hay baler. Also, having irrigation sprinklers that resemble water cannons will help to make it grow. Some really good-quality hay might even be able to make a third cut if you have enough water. Or try a method of restoration; let the animals eat it.

Farmers offering services to cut and bale your hay are concerned with quality because the more hay there is on the field, the better it is for them since they get paid a certain amount per bale. I'm not saying you should restore your hay field if the animals you are going to keep can eat the kind of hay that is growing in the field, but horses can only eat top-quality hay that is free from invasive species such as knapweed. Pigs can be fed from what you have for them, and goats and sheep can clear off an entire area of the field even with the knapweed, and they fertilize the site at the same time.

During the heat, the chickens will often go inside the chicken house to get out of the sun. It is important to make sure the chickens have a good supply of water; give them fresh food and water every day. It is important to have food and water available first thing in the morning since chickens are active and hungry as soon as it becomes light each day. Problems can definitely arise while raising chickens if you don't think beforehand about how a rooster behaves. You will find that if you have more than one rooster, they fight with each other and possibly even kill each other. People at the food store can tell you a little each time you are there. Chickens often have bad behavior, especially the roosters. So it should be good to have chickens and a vegetable garden, and you will have food year-round.

Be sure to consider changing your mind about a lot of ways you think things will happen; more so within yourself is where the success can happen. You will not know if you do not try. Be sure to spend time inside the chicken house watching what they are doing. Will you look at it as a bigger part played by the role of nature?

Document how many chickens are doing a particular thing, and make note of any different ways that they behave.

The hay field, when you investigate it, is full of potential. The hay feeds the animals and has many uses, such as mulching to protect plants from freezing and nesting boxes for chickens. The more the use of the land is switched around, the more productive it becomes. I am planning to have a circle of breeding animals that create food; they will also fertilize the land. As the animals are moved to new pasture, the land is then ready to be tilled for new gardens that add to the landscape and improve the value of the land.

Raising sheep will be the first of my breeding ventures. They don't need a large barn like bigger animals, and they don't break out of their fences as easily as goats. The females often give birth to twins so the flock will grow quickly, allowing some of the animals to be used for meat while still keeping up the numbers of the flock. Also, the meat is in high demand since it is particularly enjoyable. Sheep offer a further benefit to the land. As they graze, the grass is not torn from the ground. It is neatly packed into place as they walk over it, leaving a tidy and attractive landscape.

Watch how many foods are in store at the supermarket. It's the stores that are selling most of the food. It doesn't have to be that everyone must grow their own food so that everyone has local produce. If the economy was affordable, then it would include many small businesses to include everyone having a market for extra food. I am a general outfit that is just starting out, but once I learn, then I will be registered to teach. People would buy all the food they can, and they would have to build the product again. Everyone will be provided with all the food, especially the animals.

Excellent fertilizer comes from chicken manure as long as it is well composted. If it is too fresh, it can burn the plants roots and damage or kill the plants. The chicken manure and some added soil can be mixed and left to compost for a year prior to being added to the garden. If you are using hay in your chicken house, the extra composting time will help to kill the hay seeds. Even when you have topsoil, eventually you will need to put back into your topsoil, and then you will need to have manure or compost available to enrich it. Garden boxes are easy because they are small. You can take a hand tool to mix it in the spring. Be sure to learn about composting when you are getting started.

A completed season means you are doing very well; cultivate the chicken manure to keep the plot going year after year. Trade roosters with someone who has a different breed of chicken to keep fresh blood in your flock.

Your buildings should be dry and reasonably warm to keep your animals healthy. Also, be sure you have a storage area that is keeping the hay dry. Then maybe you will find someone to trade that hay with, if you have more than you need. You must work toward spring by creating a good working space for starting new plants and growing them into strong plants to transplant into the garden in the spring. It is also extra work to look after the animals. When it is extremely cold in the winter, make sure the animals have water that is not frozen and enough hay to eat.

There are a lot of different plant varieties to choose from. Pick some bee-friendly flowers to attract the bees to the garden because they are essential for pollenating the plants to make them produce fruit. It might be a good thing to take a bee course.

One thing to work on before you get started is to find out how to get a chicken coop going before you even have a garden of zucchinis to fertilize. If the chickens are doing their job, and they will, then you can start a garden in ground that has been cleared of weeds and fertilized, after the chickens are moved to another spot. The more workers you can pay, the easier it is to get your farm and garden producing. Is it achievable with respect to experienced help: the experienced chickens and you? Will your crew be an experienced farm at the end of the day?

Closer and closer you get to an acre that will need more chicken manure to add to the garden as it expands so you are able to try food production. The more animals I have, the more manure I have and the closer I get to an acre of tilling that the tractor needs to do in the spring. With each new addition to the garden space, I will be getting more vegetables, and I can continue to make additions if the water reaches. The main thing with the hay field is that you restore it as you go along to keep it as quality hay. When the animals are in their shelters, they can't eat off the field, so you feed them hay.

Determine a life off the land first by having chickens and prayer, and then you are living off the land once you can grow and raise your own food. Belief goes hand in hand with hardship. You will become a star by living off the land, moving from the present to the future with ambition! Living off the land isn't everybody's favorite. It needs maintenance all the time. And so, I thought, the time of my life. Doing things under the light of the cloud and in the real world.

You hear it on the news all the time. Someone has tried to control an element of nature, ending with catastrophic results. There won't be a shortage of food in the short term because it is in the stores. I don't think you can stop a shortage of food from happening; probably the elements of nature control us. The sun and the moon rise and set. When the constellations are there, the revelation is almost like doing what it always did with great control and changing with the calendar.

Coffee is grown close to the equator. If you like coffee in the morning, you can save time in the morning by not watering too much on cooler days, but the garden needs a good soaking on a hot day. Like coffee, chickens need warmth, and you don't want their water to freeze. They eat a lot in colder weather, and all year long, they eat a lot. So to help cover the cost, I use a heat lamp to keep them warm and keep them producing eggs throughout the winter. It is good for them to have lettuce or radish that has gone to seed and any other garden scraps that might be available.

No matter how busy you are on the farm, be sure to leave yourself time for a coffee break and to take care of your own personal needs. Reserve the tractor for what you are doing. This means extra work for the tractor. It may not be the idea; it may be that the work is adding up fast. Chickens can take that same manifest and make the years to come so much easier.

Collaborating is important in building barns. Couldn't you hire someone while you take care of things that you want done right away? Whether it is one, two, or three cuts per season, cutting hay requires a big enough tractor and the right equipment. When you put the hay in the nesting boxes in the chicken house, they can scratch in the hay and scratch it onto the floor. You can make a chicken coop that is a "build as you go" style as long as you can get in and out each day with food and water, even in the winter. The one that the contractor built should be able to stand for a long time. Build as you go, spending time and money as it becomes available and doing other jobs that only you can really do at that time. The thinking that I noticed is that you aren't going to get away without thinking about the chickens and everything they need. They are a very good source of food.

CHAPTER 5

SOIL

NOT EVERYWHERE YOU try to start a farm will work, but plans to begin with already cultivated land means a big purchase is required. Add a chicken house and chickens as soon as you are ready for them. You can't really guess how your day could go; it takes slow estimation. I'm sure some aspect of slow estimation eludes us in detail. It should really be, I am sure. Every different little thing I could think of, meaning benefit or reward. Accept that there is not much more than clues, even when you are at the bank to buy a property that is zoned agricultural land reserve. Everything comes down to a start.

Measuring the water is easier than measuring the plant food, even though it is important to give the seeds or seedlings the simplest measurement of water. It is easy to give them the right amount of plant food to grow green. The greening off is because the plant food given should be close to exact or right around the mark needed. Wet down the planted seed. The nursery in business always needs the right input of each member of the community so that the outcome of the business happens when it is needed most.

Higher-quality potting soil can have fewer impurities, so if you buy it by the bale at the store, then that is definitely good quality. But if you need a large quantity, you can also make your own. Choose as much sunlight as your location can offer. Again, have everything prepared ahead of time for your indoor or your outdoor planting. Carry the squash, peppers, tomatoes, and zucchini to the outdoor garden in the pots you have already transplanted them to earlier, to keep them coming along. Dig a hole with the shovel where the transplant will grow. Separate the pot from the transplant, place it in the hole, and press the soil down around the plant. Water right away, and keep in mind that the glazing you will use is to protect the delicate plant from the sun's energy.

So I should say to you as an educated estimator who is experienced and who sees it to be done: quality, quality, quality. It doesn't have to happen where I start to do any digging that I decide I don't want to dig. Let the chickens size things up when you use the tiller because the weeds are already gone. Try to perceive how the elements work out in my favor. If you really think you needed better than that, always listen to your human nature. To some amount, you might be able to count. It might not seem dry except that the potatoes really are the ones predicting how much there is to drink. If I put my effort into everything and keep going until the end of the season, I should achieve a good result. It is in the soil that starts the season, and after the season, there is getting everything ready to store.

I am going to do some thinking if I don't really believe that I know what to do, and that means I ask and am clear communicating, almost like with clear understanding. I would be able to understand even when thinking, and if I am not sure, think again. Communicating reveals even numbers when it is clear; you aren't sure because you have not done it before. I am going to do a lot of thinking about those gestures to and from rain, one particular thought at one specific time. I will reflect what I think about at another specific point in time, so then is the "star" of gestures you can count on. The soil really is the earth.

I use, for example, two pickup truck loads of composted manure to spread on the garden after the snow has melted, so it can be tilled into the soil before planting. This year, I also have a bag of dolomite lime to spread sparingly over about one half of the garden to eliminate the moss that was growing there last year. If you have chickens, they will make manure that can be added to the garden once it has been composted, and the plants will love the added nutrients. When you are first starting a garden or making a new garden box, you will want to add more manure each year; however, too much manure will supply too much nitrogen to the soil, so add only a little each year.

Write it down. Seeds that you will be starting indoors should be a variety that will transplant well enough to document. Be sure that you understand the ones you grow are like someone teaching to be clear, transplanting more than once or twice. Good fertilizer in the future is good for everyone to know you are growing healthy food. What He meant for the world He said. I believe I am being taught, except I like it when people believe me as well. I have knowledge to settle, and it is problems in my past.

As the people rise up to provide guidance, I move forward with my project cultivating my land. So in the real world, this is the power keeping us on the land. Maintaining beliefs like clockwork, it is not the same workforce as us.

For someone who works on the land, being close to the amenities is usually how they get their business done. By one measure of the morning, early morning is time to get it done. Starting the season, then starting with ripe plants by yield and how many harvests I made. Not far outside the back door is all that awesome stuff I grow myself; planting to grow is very clear to me, yet I am still working on it, working on how I can do this thing. Doing big predictions, how many rows I am going to have early on, working on how I can get my rewards. I will always be able to not worry any time I want to care. I will always believe in the power of the earth because I don't need to care while I am mixing manure. I come to life while I listen. I see those birds in the garden. They meditate just as well as anyone else could in these beautiful surroundings.

When there is a lot of moss and weeds, it chokes out the plants, so you have to remove the weeds as soon as they show up. It does seem like long ago when you first planted and did not water excessively. Too much water causes you to have missed your estimate. Counting matter in a constant equation like gestures you could see, because you really love what you are doing and you must teach them better how they gesture. Maybe what you wouldn't be without means that fellows are clearly communicating and they are remembering everything they understand better. And to start with, they wouldn't be without love.

So graduating from the first season, it's surprising how much you did there and how much food really came from there. Berries need water every day, and be sure not to forget the young fruit trees. When they sell you the sapling trees, they are learning ability, because you have to water for the first few years and scatter some manure around the tree. Then pick the fruits and prune the trees as they grow. You may also have to fence your gardens and fruit trees to keep wild animals like deer or elk from damaging them. Who will be allowed to see it? Only accept friends to see your big project and those who help you with it. Begin early on to learn, and continue to gather knowledge as time progresses until you finally become an expert gardener. Build on to the real world, and your friend who is helping you can have some ideas for networking knowledge.

It needs to happen underground, and for sure the rooting is to drink all they can, but they also need to get other things that your farm can get from chicken manure. So then the nutrients are being drawn by the root, and it goes a long way to where the root is getting the water. You want the soil to have that really good fertilizer you put underneath, so don't forget where it roots. Remember to ask someone how much you add each year. It doesn't just make the plants healthy; it helps them grow really well. Somebody would be happy to explain to you rooting underground. Will somebody explain to you how to compost or how much of it to spread over a yard?

One example of things that last over a longer period of time includes the geographic features; some mathematical features like climate are not eventual. If the cultivating of the land was done already, then the job of breaking it down would not be so hard on your equipment. If your land has not been previously cultivated, it would be better to get a plough for the tractor and then run the cultivator over the ground after it has been ploughed. Start on something that doesn't take very much time. If you have a tractor, then once the tilling is done, start with marking rows and planting them. When the nurseries make their own potting soil, they have to treat it so no weeds or bugs are in the soil. Digging in the compost is one way to think of how it works. If you dig around in the compost with a small tractor, it will be cultivated.

Just because it is an agricultural land reserve doesn't mean it is ready to plant as a garden without ground preparation. Can I start to go to work? More to the point, because you buy turnkey agricultural land, accept that I can start working right away. It is exciting seeing a tractor work that can get a big job done and ready to go! The earth needed to be changed to some extent to build towns and tools to make farms possible. I don't want to give you the wrong impression about tools either. In fact, they always need repair and maintenance.

People are out to begin in the spring or even beginning when the spring is just starting to show. I have plans to build on to it each year to come so that each year it will be a little bigger than the previous spring.

It's good to pay attention to the elements; another good way is to work on some compost. It's good to do it the very best way and safely, but in those ways. Take chickens, for example. Nothing can beat that. They make the best manure, like the elements. Like that rooster, he will be there as long as you can take care of him. The rooster is making a farm; you are a farmer, if you have chickens and vegetables. Some help with problems is a good thing like help with watering. You simply aren't getting enough time and need help so you can get enough time to rest. There could be two or three people getting work done and still getting enough time to rest, except that only I water the garden. If you have two people doing the watering, accounting for the soil wetness, the other one would be your helper. I am a lot closer to the stores now where my farm is located. When there are a few different stores not too far away, it is much easier to get another load of supplies all accounted for.

In more parts of the world, they are changing farms to modern-day equipment. In these old tractors is the blueprint to modern farms. The old ploughs drawn by horse would not have broken down very much just with several metal parts. Again, taking care of the horse meant that they needed good-quality hay.

Generally, the big greenhouse or grouping of greenhouses controls more energy there; all farms control a little bit of the energy. Counting on the soil composition is the way to predict how your plants will like it. Chicken manure will gradually turn itself into regular soil so all you have to do is add some to the garden to make it rich again, but not too rich because the plants won't like that either.

Research these days is showing as religious because the communication is that environmentalists need farming to be the answer to reverse the destructive changes and minimize the carbon footprint. The natural path to follow is from the chicken house and back to the garden. The water you get for the plants in the garden and the chickens and the farmhouse is all from the same source, which is the little creek that runs along the side of the farm.

Before the world is getting further into networking, there will be shops popping up everywhere from farmers with their own chickens. If I have a group of helpers who can make an infrastructure, then I can count that as a fortune. If it is me fighting against it, I should hire a driver even if it is for the amount of time it took for me to count myself as fortunate. Say a prayer for my dinner because I appreciate the vegetables that I have grown in my garden.

Soil is the main problem because you want it to start there early. It is using the greenhouse to grow that much more flavor. Just like it is to know about topsoil, changing the composition of the soil is furthering the experience in compost from building a nutritious compost pile to building a more nutritious soil for the garden. The agricultural land must be dug up at some point to create a garden. And you might need to see what is underneath, or before you know it, you have underground water or flooding. Science could perceive what's under the ground and you might end up with more water than you want in the early spring.

When the chickens poop in the run and make layers of compost, you can dig it out if you know what is under the compost layer. If it is just regular topsoil, you could move it or plant it right where it is after it is tilled. Then the chickens would need a new run.

It is clear they are selling produce at the farmers' market. What is for sale? Honey? Honey for sale is common at the farmers' market; the likeliness that they will have honey is because of the small farms popping up everywhere. When serious farmers come together where it is on sale, it is a social likeliness that it is time for local outlets. Like bees, social development does not spread its wings toward simply anywhere.

When it is rewarding for me, it will be with doing more—how it will happen for me! And now my ideas have become ambitions achieved! Who is doing what at what time? And when you felt glad, where were you and what were you doing? Regarding people who are not feeling like it, then it will be time to ask yourself how best to move forward. I like feeling rewarded in the sense that this is it—where I am and how I am doing it. Fertilization is to do with rain in the soil because the mixture of the soil must happen as well as the rain, and it needs to happen right away. If you won't get it mixed before it rains, you want the soil wet so you must water if it isn't raining. The mixtures are happening year-round. Also, the elements are mixing.

Hand-to-eye coordination comes into play, and before you know it, you are looking like a gardener. The walkways and the rows altogether will be cleared of weeds with a tool. You are the one who is going to fit there in the walkways, so I wouldn't say if the walkways should be wide or narrow. No matter how they are managed, the plants have to be able to root in ground that is not being walked on. I understand for myself how far apart they are planted. In the plot, the crops will use a lot more area when they are big and that needs to be factored in. Also, how much garden hose room do you have? Several yards over in one corner could need water even though it is tricky to get there. It is not as warm, so you think in the spring when the plant is still very small. Don't overwater so they don't get wet and cold, or try using a hotbed.

Try to count a sense of how it will happen and how it will be and then where I should be when vegetables need tending. Vegetables would give me a certain feeling at a certain time. "They like it right away" is what I should say to you. Everyone believes in how you comprehend something you make. When things can be made, you can make those things again into prayer. It came from there in the first place, but you should try to put as much back in as you take out. Wouldn't that be the natural thing? Once I see how I am doing first thing in the morning, I know where I should be: in the garden with the tap on.

Hand tools that make the job possible and make the job go quicker and easier are essential. After doing a lot of weeding, you may feel tired all over your body and want the sauna; helping someone could make anyone tired and want the sauna. There is such a thing as a hand-weeding tool and several methods to weeding. Look forward to raising the bar for yourself every season. You should never have to think you won't. Raise the bar, and document harvest dates. Maybe I can try to notice climate change, including the people doing more about it. I can become an environmentalist and discover who really matters and accept them for it.

Just do the *big* job when I am up to it, but because it is such a big job, sometimes it gets to where I need help. Garden boxes and small gardens can be done with hand tools. Try out your compost in the garden boxes, and put chicken manure at the bottom of the cold frame to add warmth for the plants so it becomes a hotbed. If you don't have access to topsoil, you can buy potting soil in bales at the garden center to fill your garden boxes or your cold frames. Another way to do it would be to buy a truckload of topsoil and fill the area from that. So then buying soil will fill up the different kinds of boxes. Start a new garden or expand your existing garden. A hotbed, if you know how to build one, is a very good way to get an early start in the garden.

A flower garden will have a better chance over winter if insulated with maple leaves. Cherry tomatoes are done when the last ones are picked. When they are kept under a roof at night, they will survive through frost that would usually damage them. So you see the elements will work for you in some cases, and in other cases, the soil can work against you. You won't be able to control what will happen during the season. Except a tractor will help you achieve the goals that you are reaching for, so it is a very big tractor that would do a big job. A big greenhouse project or a small greenhouse project, you can always count on your tractor.

Certain goals, I believe, should be met. When I look to my next thing to learn, I require something to work on. "Are there certain goals?" I asked myself before I got started the very first time, and at the same time, I was piling rows because I saw it in a picture. So just go ahead and build up the rows in the plot—nice, big, raised rows. That is the prediction I counted on earlier, when I first thought about it long ago, before my first season. I found out later that with potatoes, it is best to plant them and pile up the rows later when it is time to hill them. As long as I keep learning, I am making progress; don't try to teach anything you can't count on. Accept that vegetables have a certain science behind satisfaction divided into one garden that is secretive.

Generous application of earth and manure is taught commonly by people who are trying to run greenhouses.

That is how you want the fences to go, but they aren't saying how heavy the tomatoes are going to be when they grow in the greenhouse. Sunlight is what makes it grow. It will thrive there when the elements are glowing like with any impressive rain. Amounts of these elements and generous amounts of nutrients are done best in the greenhouse. That doesn't mean you don't have to protect them; the greenhouse is there to protect them when they are being transplanted or when the tomatoes are hanging from the vines.

CHAPTER 6

COMPOST

KITCHEN WASTE BUILDS up to a whopping amount of compost, but the main one is the chicken manure from the chicken coop to make it grow best for anything you want. I don't know why you wouldn't want to have chickens. They have to be able to have chicks to keep the flock going, and the more chickens you raise, the bigger the garden patch will become. Mulching is a possibility for using leaves, and come spring, the mulch can be removed from the gardens and added to the compost pile. Maple leaves in particular are an excellent addition to compost. Whatever goes back into the compost should be the best material to make the best compost possible to improve your garden once it has composted sufficiently. It is important to turn the compost pile over a few times during the gardening season to help it break down more thoroughly. If you can use a tractor to till it, that is quicker and easier than doing it by hand.

If you have grounds to have chickens, then you must have chickens because you will then have such a beautiful garden. In the morning, it could be a good time to shovel compost while you have the water running in other parts of the garden. The morning is watering time, but no one can say you don't know what is going on even if you are facing the compost pile that is being used to do those things unless your chickens aren't pooping. Be sure to do what Farmer John would do; he would raise a flock of chickens in a chicken house. While you are turning the compost, you can see how much it has broken down into soil. Chickens like the sun, and they like to be dry. When it is cold or raining, you will find them inside the chicken house. It doesn't seem that hard to learn. I could set a goal to be the star of making my own soil, and it doesn't seem that hard after all.

One subject that goes overlooked is the big jobs. When turning the compost, easy does it. This small detail or subject goes overlooked because the neighbor who brought it in a truckload seeks it everywhere. Chicken manure is the best way to make your own soil the way that it has been done before. Getting hay seeds mixed up in your compost pile causes a problem, for example, because you need to compost it for one extra season to make sure all the weeds don't end up in your garden. It needs a good mixing a few times during the season to be sure it breaks down evenly and all the seeds have been killed.

Many things can be added to the compost pile, such as lawn clippings, leaves, weeds that have been pulled from the garden, and any hay that has been used for mulch or animal bedding. To keep the floor of the chicken house from rotting, it can be cleaned regularly and added to a new compost pile that can wait an extra season before being added back into the garden.

To reference the Bible, there is not a time when one shouldn't be gardening. To grow food is to be close to God; believing is the one true fundamental fact. And the truth is no matter how it can be so, it's your place in life. How is the earth connected with heaven? And connection with the earth is the main one to know.

Printed in the United States
by Baker & Taylor Publisher Services